The Great Fire of London
Was it inevitable?

Contents

T0318095

Written by Liz Miles

Collins

1 Introduction

Why was it called the "Great Fire"?

The Great Fire of London is named "Great" because it was so big and destroyed around a third of London – the capital of England and one of the world's largest cities. Thousands of homes were burnt down, and hundreds of people probably died.

This book discusses:

- What caused the fire?

- Why did it spread?

Think about the questions as you read the book, so you can come up with your own opinion of what happened.

How do we find the answers?

We can look for evidence in sources like people's diaries, government records, pictures and maps of London. Modern research offers clues, too.

Each source needs careful thought. Ask yourself questions like these:

- Is this a fact or just one person's opinion?

- Can this writer be trusted?

- Is the picture factual or based on the artist's ideas?

A model of 1660s London was set alight to mark the 350th anniversary of the fire in 2016.

2 What was London like before the fire?

Maps and records show that in the 1660s, London was much smaller than today but it was a busy, crowded place (around 350,000 people lived there). The Great Fire affected two main parts, north of the River Thames:

- the City of London
- the City of Westminster.

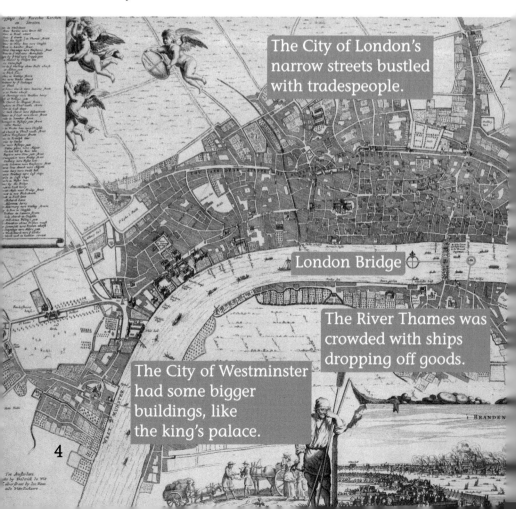

The City of London's narrow streets bustled with tradespeople.

London Bridge

The River Thames was crowded with ships dropping off goods.

The City of Westminster had some bigger buildings, like the king's palace.

4

Look at this illustration of London at the time – what might catch fire easily, or help the fire to spread?

The City of London and London Bridge had tightly packed buildings.

wooden frames

The Great Plague

Before the fire, London had suffered a tragedy.
A deadly **plague** killed about one in every five people
in 1665. Londoners were nervous that the plague
might come back.

A city of fires

There was no electricity or gas in the 17th century.
For light, people used candles. To keep warm
and cook, they lit fires in **hearths** or ovens. A candle,
or spark from a fire often set light to things nearby.
Fires in towns and cities were common, but they were
usually put out quickly with buckets of water.

London's Globe Theatre,
where the famous playwright
William Shakespeare
worked, was burnt
down in a fire in 1613.
Cannons fired during
a play set fire to it.

London had overhanging buildings like these – do you think they might burn easily?

7

A disaster waiting to happen?

People knew that fires could easily spread in London. In 1665, King Charles warned the lord mayor of the danger because of the narrow streets and wooden, overhanging houses.

The City of London was crammed with wooden buildings.

Look at the diagram and ask yourself these questions:

- What made fires more likely in London? Why?
- What might have made a small fire spread? Why?
- How dangerous was London in 1666?

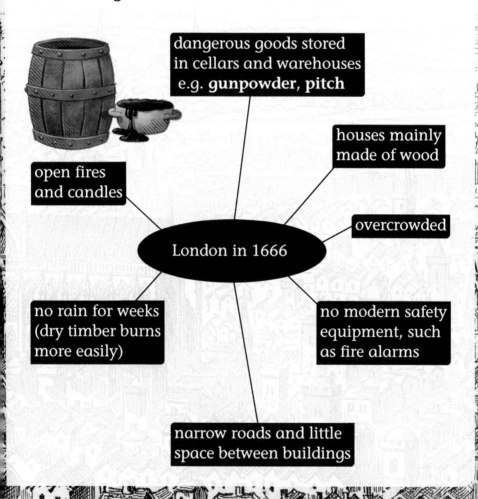

dangerous goods stored in cellars and warehouses e.g. **gunpowder, pitch**

houses mainly made of wood

open fires and candles

overcrowded

London in 1666

no rain for weeks (dry timber burns more easily)

no modern safety equipment, such as fire alarms

narrow roads and little space between buildings

3 How did the fire start?

Most people agree on a basic timeline of events for the Great Fire. A lot of information comes from a committee which recorded **witness statements** after the fire. But there are still lots of questions to ask – can we always completely trust witness statements?

Sunday 2nd September 1666 – the fire begins

Witness statements said the fire started early on Sunday morning in a bakery in Pudding Lane. Perhaps a spark from an oven set flour sacks or wood on fire? Thomas Farriner, the baker, later explained that he, his daughter and **manservant** were woken by a fire at about 1 o'clock and escaped from an upstairs window.

The baker lit a fire in the oven and shut the door. When it was hot enough, he cleared away the fire and put the bread in to cook. Each night, he had to check the fire was out.

By 3 o'clock, witnesses reported hearing drumming –
a warning to everyone nearby.

They said the lord mayor of London came to look.
People asked him if they could demolish nearby
houses to stop the fire from spreading. But he said no –
he was worried about who would pay to rebuild them.
He said it was a small fire and went home. Why do
you think he made that decision?

Recently, **archaeologists** found remains of barrels of
pitch from the fire, in cellars in Pudding Lane.

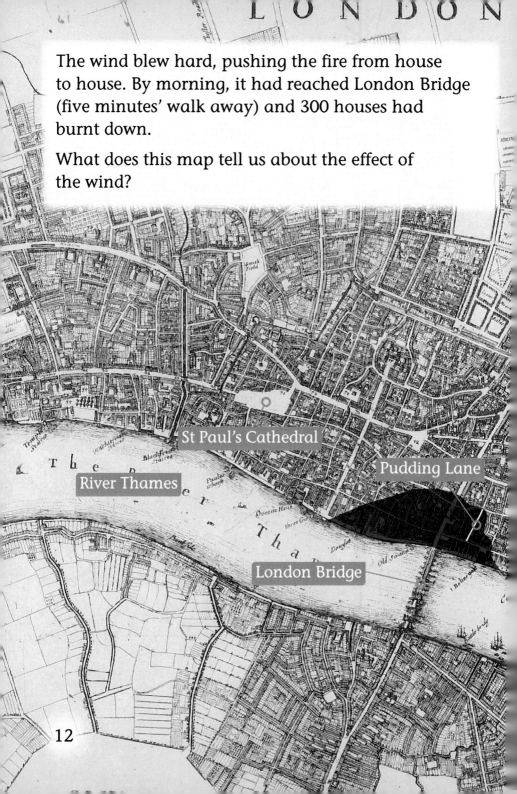

The wind blew hard, pushing the fire from house to house. By morning, it had reached London Bridge (five minutes' walk away) and 300 houses had burnt down.

What does this map tell us about the effect of the wind?

St Paul's Cathedral

Pudding Lane

River Thames

London Bridge

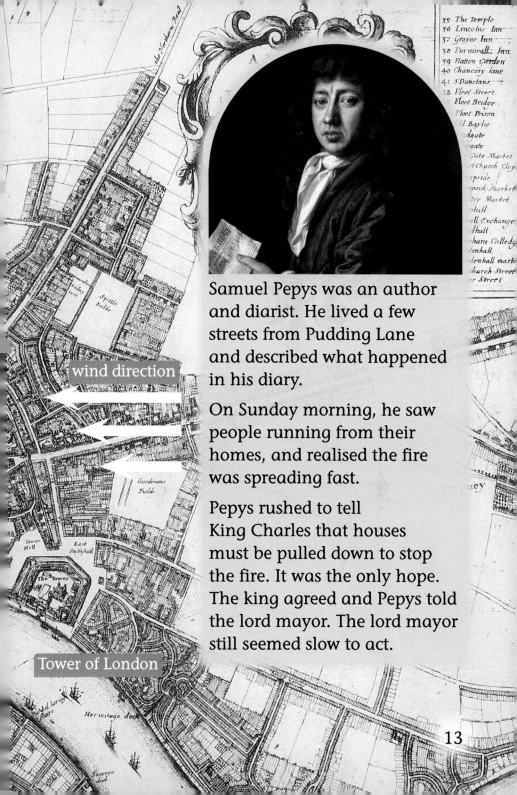

wind direction

Tower of London

Samuel Pepys was an author and diarist. He lived a few streets from Pudding Lane and described what happened in his diary.

On Sunday morning, he saw people running from their homes, and realised the fire was spreading fast.

Pepys rushed to tell King Charles that houses must be pulled down to stop the fire. It was the only hope. The king agreed and Pepys told the lord mayor. The lord mayor still seemed slow to act.

4 How did it spread?

Monday 3rd September

Witnesses described how on Monday, as the fire spread along the riverbank and up into the city, panic filled the streets.

The king put his brother, the Duke of York, in charge of stopping the fire's spread. He set up eight fire posts all around the fire. Thirty soldiers and 100 volunteers worked hard from each post.

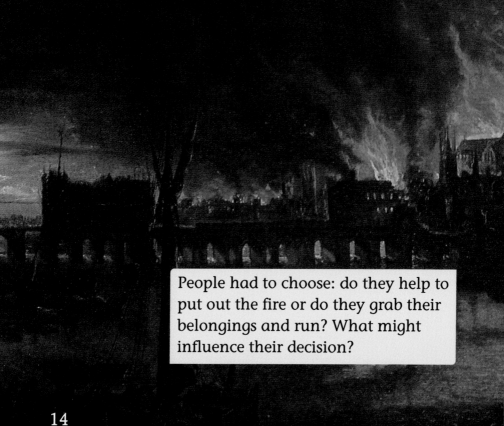

People had to choose: do they help to put out the fire or do they grab their belongings and run? What might influence their decision?

John Evelyn worked in
the king's court. On Monday, he
wrote in his diary that he saw:

the sky looked fiery

it burnt ... it leapt from street
to street

He heard:

the hurrying of people
and the falling of towers

How do you think Evelyn may
have felt?

Witness statements describe how fighting the fire got harder. The streets were crowded with carts and it was difficult to drag the fire engines to the flames. Water to put out the fire was pumped from the river.

LONDON

Pudding Lane

St Paul's Cathedral

River Thames

London Bridge

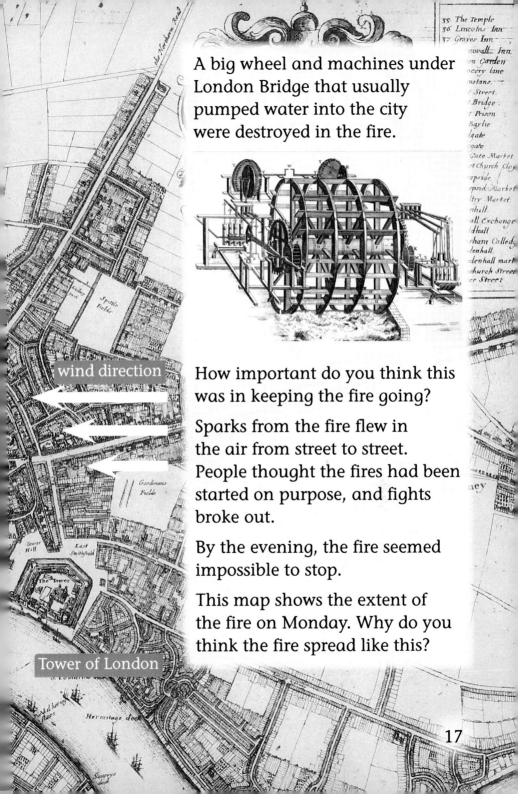

A big wheel and machines under London Bridge that usually pumped water into the city were destroyed in the fire.

How important do you think this was in keeping the fire going?

Sparks from the fire flew in the air from street to street. People thought the fires had been started on purpose, and fights broke out.

By the evening, the fire seemed impossible to stop.

This map shows the extent of the fire on Monday. Why do you think the fire spread like this?

wind direction

Tower of London

Firefighting equipment

In 1666, local people in London only had basic equipment that was stored in a church in each area.

Compare this equipment with modern fire engines and firefighting eqiuipment.

Pickaxes
People used pickaxes to break open water pipes to fill their buckets.

Leather buckets and ladders
Buckets had to be carried up ladders and tipped into burning buildings.

Firehooks
Long firehooks were used to tug down burning roof tiles or timber house frames.

What is a firebreak?

Buildings were pulled down beside a fire to cause a firebreak so the flames had nowhere to spread, and nothing to burn. Do you think firebreaks helped stop the Great Fire?

Fire squirt

These metal, hand-held pumps shot water into the flames.

Fire engines

These early fire engines broke or were too hard to drag down the narrow lanes.

How it worked

A short hose didn't reach far.

The barrel was filled with buckets of water.

These Engins, (which are ...... the best) to quench great Fires; are

JOHN KEELING

People pumped the handles to move the water into the hose.

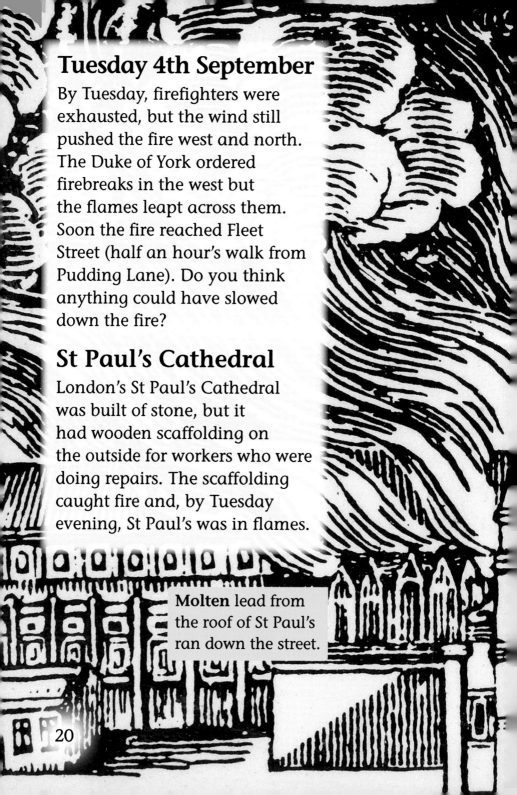

Tuesday 4th September

By Tuesday, firefighters were exhausted, but the wind still pushed the fire west and north. The Duke of York ordered firebreaks in the west but the flames leapt across them. Soon the fire reached Fleet Street (half an hour's walk from Pudding Lane). Do you think anything could have slowed down the fire?

St Paul's Cathedral

London's St Paul's Cathedral was built of stone, but it had wooden scaffolding on the outside for workers who were doing repairs. The scaffolding caught fire and, by Tuesday evening, St Paul's was in flames.

Molten lead from the roof of St Paul's ran down the street.

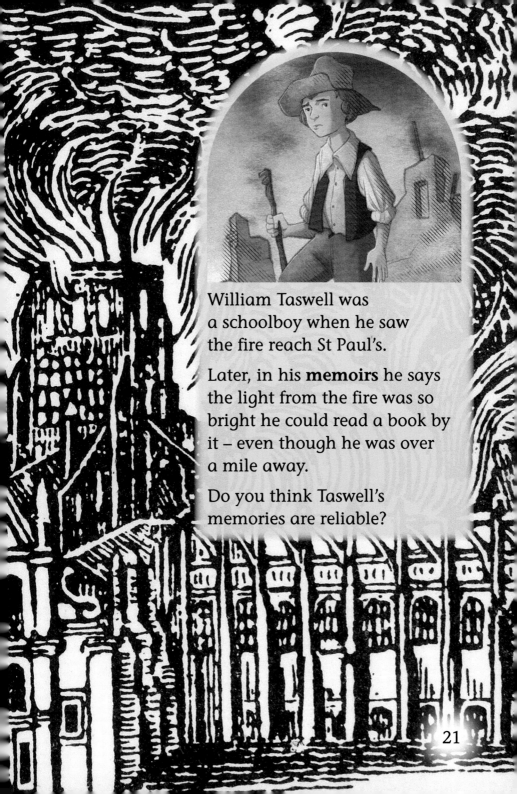

William Taswell was a schoolboy when he saw the fire reach St Paul's.

Later, in his **memoirs** he says the light from the fire was so bright he could read a book by it – even though he was over a mile away.

Do you think Taswell's memories are reliable?

How did people behave?

Witnesses described how people ran from the city, and **looters** grabbed what they could from empty shops and houses.

What do you think this image shows? Why did thousands leave their belongings behind when they **fled** the fire?

Buried treasure

Like many rich people, Pepys sent his money and silver away in a cart in case the fire reached his house.

William Taswell wrote that his father was robbed by someone pretending to help.

Gunpowder

To the east, the fire advanced more slowly.
Why do you think it was slower in this direction?
Eventually, it got close to the Tower of London,
so soldiers used gunpowder and cannons to blow
up nearby houses to form firebreaks. The fire was
stopped just as it reached the tower gates.

Look at the map. How fierce do you think the fire
was at this stage? Why?

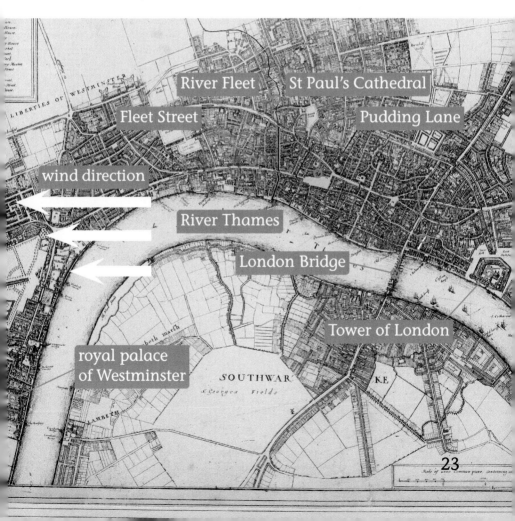

River Fleet

St Paul's Cathedral

Fleet Street

Pudding Lane

wind direction

River Thames

London Bridge

Tower of London

royal palace
of Westminster

SOUTHWARK

5 How did the fire stop?

Wednesday 5th September

On Wednesday, the wind stopped blowing and the fire stopped spreading so quickly. At last, firefighters had the chance to extinguish the fire. Most of the City of London was in ruins.

On Wednesday morning, Pepys climbed up a church steeple and described "the saddest sight of desolation" he had ever seen. Fires seemed to burn everywhere.

John Evelyn recorded, as early as Tuesday, seeing crowds of people who had been made homeless living in tents, huts and **hovels**.

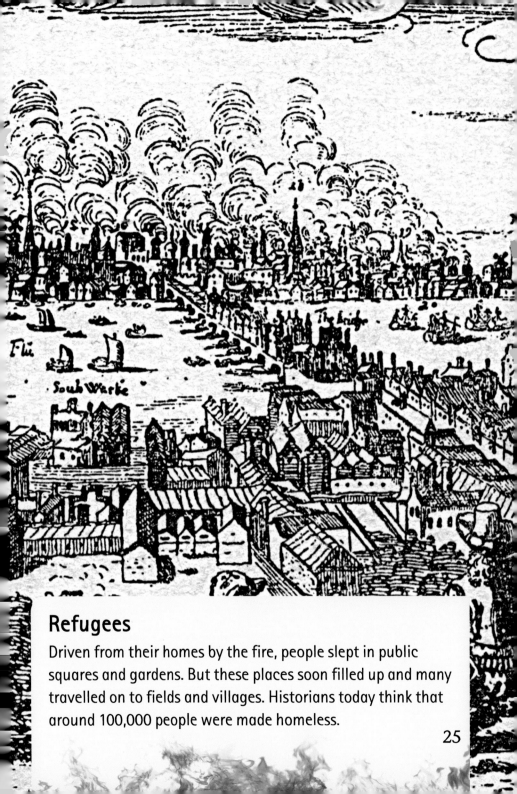

Refugees

Driven from their homes by the fire, people slept in public squares and gardens. But these places soon filled up and many travelled on to fields and villages. Historians today think that around 100,000 people were made homeless.

25

Thursday 6th September

The Great Fire of London was over, but the clean-up had to begin.

An army of 200 men from outside London were called in to help clear the streets of **debris** and pour water on any smoking ruins.

This picture of the ruins after the fire was printed much later, in 1792. Do you think this is an accurate picture of the devastation? Why?

William Taswell remembered clambering over the smoking ruins of St Paul's on Thursday, where he saw just heaps of stones and molten metal bells.

6 What do you think?

Who do we believe?

Samuel Pepys and John Evelyn gave first-hand accounts of the fire in their diaries. They tell us how the fire looked, felt and even smelt. But some of their accounts might have been muddled. Pepys wrote that he almost forgot what day it was! With the sky lit by fire every night, and the constant roar of the flames, keeping a diary was difficult.

William Taswell was a schoolboy when he saw the fire. He wrote about the fire years afterwards. Was his memory reliable? Or perhaps the experience was so shocking, every detail stayed clear in his mind?

Would it be easy to write a diary with this around you?

This is a mural of a painting that shows people escaping from the Great Fire of London. The artist finished it in 1898, over 200 years after the fire. Do you think it could be realistic?

Who caused the fire?

Most people believe the fire started in Thomas Farriner's bakery. Was the baker himself to blame? Did he forget to put out his oven fire?

Records show that Thomas Farriner got into trouble as a boy. He was taken to Billingsgate Prison (a place where "stray" children were kept and educated).

After the Great Fire, Thomas Farriner claimed that on the night the fire began:

- The fire in the bakehouse oven had been put out at 10 o'clock.

- At midnight, he checked it and there wasn't enough heat left to light a candle.

- He checked all windows and doors were shut so no draught could fan any fires.

- Lastly, he went to bed.

He also said that all the dry wood in the oven was found after the fire, unburnt, so the fire didn't start in his bakery.

How reliable is Thomas Farriner's account?

Blaming people

Lots of different people were blamed for starting the fire on purpose. Wars with the Netherlands and France meant that Dutch and French people in London were picked on and blamed for the fire.

Fifty witness statements were collected to find the cause of the fire. In the end, the king claimed that the fire was caused by the "hand of god" and the wind and dry weather.

An angry crowd attacked a man when they thought some tennis balls he carried were fireballs.

Cozen Goddard

I being on the 16th of September last sent for by me
own Phillips my Client to the Savoy where he had then
newly taken possession of an house wherein Mr Anthony
Shorter had some few dayes before dwelt and which me
Phillips recovered from the said Mr Shorter who is a
Chirurgeon & a Frenchman & a reputed papist I went
after dinner thither and when I came there I found in one
roome two bundles of long reed severall of which had
fireworkes tyed to them. The fireworkes were of severall
sorts & divers shapes some being wrapped up in fine linen
some greater some lesse still others in pastboard, haveing great heads with abundance
of lesser workes in the heads made with pastboard others
haveing abundance of Quills filled with fireworkes I asked
what they were for, and Mr Phillips man said that not long
before there were ten tymes as many but what was become
of them they know not I asked some who seemed to be Mr
Shorters servants what use they were made for because
they were very suspicious and they answered they were
made against the Thanksgiving for the peace, but they
seemed to have beene made a good while, I did see some
of them fired singly. for they durst not fire them in
that manner as they were made and they burnt very
violently, especially that which was wrapped in ragg and
the bodys of those wrapped up in pastboard burnt all the
tyme it was there which was above halfe an houre, some of
them I brought with me & shewed you, God knowes the
true end they were made for, this is all I know and all
I saw Mr Phillips lives in Drury lane, for who with his
man were there I wondered what to see them that house
for I know Mr Shorter was a surgeon & dealt with
wines and not in fireworkes, soe I rest

yor loving friend

Robert Goddard   Tho: Peachell

One witness statement suggested that
the fire was part of a Catholic plot to
damage London.

Why did the fire burn for so long?

Lots of people did their best to put out the fire, so why wasn't the fire stopped sooner? Which of these do you think was most important in keeping the fire burning?

Stored goods

Lots of flammable goods, like oil, gunpowder and pitch were stored in cellars for safekeeping. Goods like paper and books were hidden in churches during the disaster. All these added fuel to the fire.

Wind

The narrow streets were like funnels, forcing the wind faster, which pushed the flames along.

William Taswell said that the wind carried burning embers three furlongs (about the length of six football pitches, end to end)

Dry weather

It had not rained for weeks so the timber buildings were dry and burnt quickly.

Intense heat

The firefighters' firesquirts and hoses did not reach very far and the heat was intense.

7 What happened after the fire?

How many lost lives?

Records from the time show fewer than ten deaths but surely many more people died in the crowded houses? About 13,200 houses were destroyed, which probably left around 100,000 people homeless.

Rich and poor people lived side by side, after losing their homes.

Did the fire cost money?

As well as houses, many public buildings were burnt down, including:

- St Paul's Cathedral
- 87 of London's 109 churches
- Newgate Prison
- 52 halls of livery companies (trade headquarters).

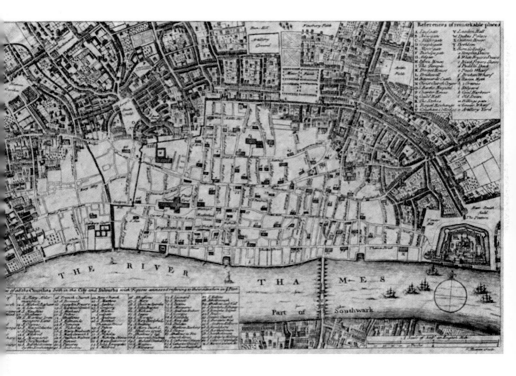

This map, drawn in 1667, shows the wasteland of ruins left after the fire.

Lessons learnt

What lessons do you think were learnt? What changes could be made to a city like London to stop a fire spreading like that again? Let's see what they did.

King Charles told planners that, if possible, streets had to be wider so flames could not cross over them so quickly.

The Act for the Rebuilding of the City of London in 1667 laid down new rules. It said:

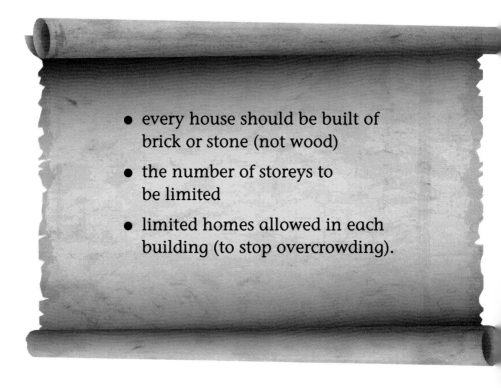

- every house should be built of brick or stone (not wood)
- the number of storeys to be limited
- limited homes allowed in each building (to stop overcrowding).

In the Great Fire, people had to smash water pipes to fill their buckets! Afterwards, holes with lids were put on water pipes to make it easier to get the water. Every area had to have more firefighting equipment ready, too.

the remains of a leather fire bucket from the 1600s, similar to those used on the fire

Why was rebuilding London important?

While London was in ruins, trade and more money was lost, and thousands of people lived in shacks and tents.

Records show that by the end of 1670, 6,000 houses had been rebuilt, but the ruined churches took longer.

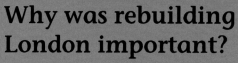

Public buildings like churches were rebuilt with money from a new **coal tax**.

St Paul's Cathedral

Architect Christopher Wren designed and supervised the new St Paul's. The giant dome was like a symbol of London rising again from the ashes.

Christopher Wren became a "Sir" when he was knighted for his help in rebuilding London.

8 Summing up

You have looked at a lot of information and evidence about the fire, including witness statements, facts from records of the time, maps and pictures. Which sources of information do you think are the most reliable?

Many people think that the fire started in the bakery off Pudding Lane. Do you think it was the baker's fault? Why? Why not?

There are many theories as to why the Great Fire of London spread so far. What's your view?

Look at this word cloud and consider:

- Who made mistakes?

- Who made good decisions?

- What made the fire worse?

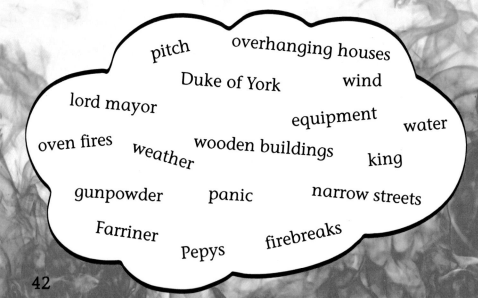

pitch   overhanging houses
Duke of York   wind
lord mayor   equipment   water
oven fires   weather   wooden buildings   king
gunpowder   panic   narrow streets
Farriner   firebreaks
Pepys

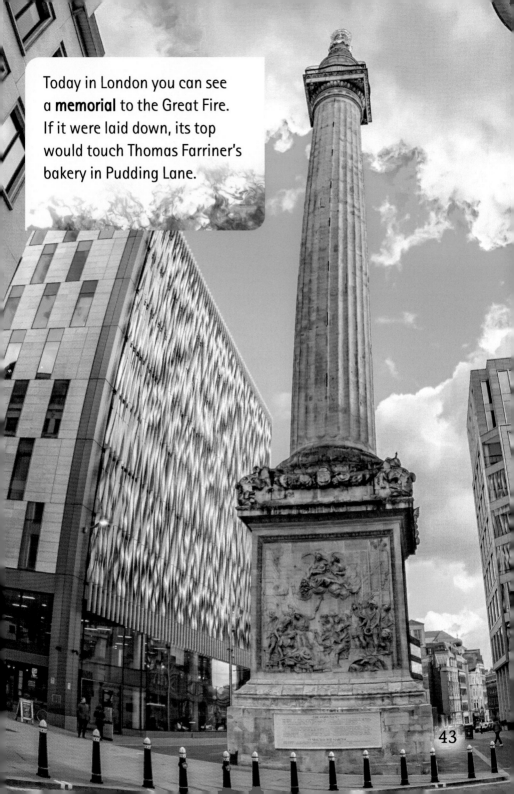

Today in London you can see a **memorial** to the Great Fire. If it were laid down, its top would touch Thomas Farriner's bakery in Pudding Lane.

43

Glossary

archaeologists people who dig up old objects to study

coal tax extra money people paid when they bought coal, which went to the government

debris remains, such as bits of burnt wood, from a building

fled ran away or escaped

gunpowder a powder that explodes if you set light to it

hearths the floors around fireplaces

hovels small dirty huts or houses where people lived

looters thieves, especially during a disaster

manservant a male servant

memoirs a written account of what the writer remembers from his or her past

memorial a building or statue to remind people of an event or person

molten turned to liquid because of great heat

pitch highly flammable thick, black substance for waterproofing

plague a disease that spread quickly and killed many people in the past

witness statements written or spoken reports on what someone saw; the witness usually has to promise to tell the truth

Index

Consider the sources ...

Which of these witnesses do you think is
the most reliable? Why?

Thomas Farriner

William Taswell

Samuel Pepys

John Evelyn

Ideas for reading

Written by Christine Whitney
Primary Literacy Consultant

Reading objectives:
- be introduced to non-fiction books that are structured in different ways
- listen to, discuss and express views about non-fiction
- retrieve and record information from non-fiction
- discuss and clarify the meanings of words

Spoken language objectives:
- participate in discussion
- speculate, hypothesise, imagine and explore ideas through talk
- ask relevant questions

Curriculum links: History: Develop an awareness of the past; Writing: Write for different purposes

Word count: 3160

Interest words: flammable, funnels, timber, intense, eyewitness

Resources: paper, pencils and crayons, access to the internet, recyclable materials for model building

Build a context for reading

- Ask children what they already know about the Great Fire of London. What questions do they have about the Great Fire?
- Look closely at the front cover and discuss what can be seen. Say that this is a model of London, that was burnt to commemorate the anniversary of the fire.
- Read the blurb and ask for a volunteer to explain what an *eyewitness* is. Would the group trust an *eyewitness* account?

Understand and apply reading strategies

- Read together up to the end of Chapter 2. Ask children to summarise why it was thought that the Great Fire of London was a *disaster waiting to happen.*
- Continue to read Chapters 3 and 4. Look carefully at the illustrations showing the equipment firefighters had in 1666. Ask children to explain why this was not sufficient to stop the fire.